Streets of Belfast

Mark Kennedy

Ian Allan
PUBLISHING

Introduction

Whilst the focus of this book is the portrayal, in colour, of Belfast's trams, buses and trolleybuses in the 20 or so years after the end of the Second World War, it is my hope that it will also convey something of the wider atmosphere of the city in this period, especially the 1950s and 1960s when the majority of the photographs were taken.

In response to the urban transport needs of the rapidly expanding city, horse-drawn trams first began operating in Belfast in 1872. Electric trams replaced them in 1905 when ownership of the network passed to Belfast Corporation. At first the system worked very well, but by the 1930s, it was clear that trams were really not compatible with the increasing levels of private motor traffic in the city. Trams normally travelled along the centre of the road, which was fine when they shared that road with relatively slow moving horse-drawn vehicles. As motor traffic increased the problems of traffic congestion and the danger to passengers, entering and leaving the trams in the centre of the road, grew.

The Corporation decided to introduce electric-powered trolleybuses to replace the trams. The wires from which the trolleybuses took their power supply could be attached to the existing poles which suppported the overhead wires used by the trams. Unlike trams, they could pull over and stop at the kerb to allow passengers to board and alight in safety, though one drawback they shared with the trams was that they could not overtake one another.

The changeover from trams to trolleybuses was interrupted by the outbreak of war in 1939. By the early 1950s, diesel motor buses had become more economical to run and offered a more flexible option than the trolleybuses. By now the tram fleet was old and virtually worn out, some of the vehicles having been in operation for almost 50 years. The final curtain on the trams came down on Saturday 28 February 1954. Whilst the network of trolleybus routes continued to be extended — eventually Belfast had the second largest trolleybus fleet in the United Kingdom — the inflexibility of vehicles tied to their overhead wires and a fleet now showing its age, led in the 1960s to the decision to abandon the trolleybuses. The number of routes served by trolleybuses was progressively reduced and the last trolleybuses ran in Belfast on Sunday 12 May 1968.

In the early postwar period, colour film was still expensive and sometimes difficult to obtain. Nevertheless, with the help of many fellow transport enthusiasts, I have been able to bring together an interesting collection of photographs from this period covering many parts of the city. My thanks are due to the photographers for their foresight in recording these scenes in colour. They are; Robert Beggs, Wilfred Capper, I. Davidson, Clifton Flewitt, William Holden, Reg Ludgate, William Montgomery, William Robb MBE, W. E. Roberson, Richard Whitford. Thanks also go to Ron White for access to the extensive Colour Rail archive. My task was made much easier thanks to the help and assistance of Andrew Anderson, Kenneth Anderson, the Ulster Folk & Transport Museum, the Auld family, Bryan Boyle, Tom Ferris, the Friel family, Mike Maybin, Maureen Paige and Pat and Debra Wenlock.

So join me on this journey through Belfast's recent past. You will enter a more relaxed world where there was much less traffic than today and life seemed to be less hectic. I hope you enjoy the trip.

Mark Lynd Kennedy
Groomsport, 2003

Front cover: A Daimler Fleetline bus, No 657, at Donegall Square East. The classical building to the right was Donegall Square Methodist Church. It is now the Ulster Bank.

Back cover: A McCreary tram passing Gilpin Bros, gent's outfitters, as it turns the corner from Donegall Square North into Donegall Place.

Previous page: Royal Avenue, with the three variants of public transport in the city, a double-decker omnibus, a tram and a trolleybus.
Colour-Rail/W. E. Robertson (IR345)

This book is dedicated to the memory of Alfred Montgomery and Bryan Boyle.

First published 2003

ISBN 0 7110 2959 8

Published by Ian Allan Publishing
an imprint of Ian Allan Publishing Ltd, Hersham, Surrey KT12 4RG.
Printed by Ian Allan Printing Ltd, Hersham, Surrey KT12 4RG.

Code: 0311/B

Chamberlain tram No 357 and Mc Creary car No 397 are seen at the Ligoniel terminus. The tram depot was around the corner to the left. The Chamberlain tram was one of 50 ordered in 1930. It was customary for new designs to bear the names of the General Manager of the time, hence Chamberlains and McCrearys after William Chamberlain and Lt-Col R. McCreary. The Chamberlain cars, Nos 342-391, carried a new blue and cream livery. They were fitted with sprung seats covered in brown leather and had electric heaters. No 357 has been preserved and is on display at the Ulster Folk & Transport Museum at Cultra.
Colour-Rail

Left: A 1942 AEC trolleybus and a Guy double-decker bus in Donegall Square North. The Linenhall Library can be seen to the left of the red sandstone building. The library building was built for linen manufacturers in 1864 and adapted for use as a library in 1896 when the White Linen Hall was demolished to make way for the new City Hall and the library needed new premises. The motorcars in the photograph are an Austin A40 and a Simca Aronde. *Colour-Rail*

Below: A trolleybus passes the statue of Sir Edward Carson in front of the Parliament Buildings at Stormont. Carson, a Dublin barrister famous for his cross-examination of Oscar Wilde, was the leader of the Ulster Unionists during the home rule controversy between 1911 and 1921. Although he opposed Home Rule, he also strongly disliked partition. He died in 1935 and is the only person buried in St Anne's Cathedral in Belfast. Parliament Buildings was built of Mourne granite and Portland stone to house the Northern Ireland parliament. It was opened by the Prince of Wales in November 1932. The blue Ulster Transport Authority coach in front of the buildings was one of those which ran tours to places, 'of interest and beauty', such as the Giant's Causeway and the Glens of Antrim. *Colour-Rail*

Below: Chamberlain tram No 359 and an unidentified trolleybus are seen at Castle Junction. To the left is the Bank Buildings, named after a previous building on the site. It was one of the first steel-framed buildings in the city and home to Robertson, Ledlie, Ferguson & Company's department store. It was constructed with brown polished granite imported from Sweden and red Dumfries sandstone. To the right of it is the Provincial Bank of Ireland, completed in the 1860s to the designs of William Barre. This is a fine example of neo-classical building spiced up with details in the then-fashionable gothic style. It is now a Tesco supermarket.
Colour-Rail (IR341)

Right: A 1948 Guy trolleybus passes Saint Anne's Cathedral in Donegall Street. The cathedral was under construction for most of the 20th century. When the north transept was finished in 1981, the cathedral was deemed to have been completed. However, it still lacks a spire. Each Christmas, since the mid-1980s there has been a famous charity vigil outside the cathedral. This was started by Dean Crooks and earned him, and his successors, the affectionate nickname, 'Black Santa' because of the heavy black woollen cape he wore. The car park beside the cathedral has been replaced by gardens, part of the revitalization of the the whole area around the building in recent years. The destination blind on the trolleybus is showing route No 6 for Bellevue. This was Belfast's 'mountain' playground. The Corporation Transport department acquired 40 acres at Bellevue when they purchased the Cavehill & Whitewell Tramway in 1910. Among the attractions at Bellevue was the Floral Hall for dancing, a narrow gauge railway, golf, donkey rides and band concerts and most famously, Belfast zoo. Belfast Corporation was unique in being the only tram operator to own its own zoo, a great source of banter at annual tram operators conferences.
Colour-Rail

Left: The location is Carr's Glen on the Ballysillan Road with Cavehill in the background. A trolleybus on route No 33, Cregagh via Cliftonville Road and Albert Bridge, passes a Daimler diesel double decker on route No 83 to Ormeau. George Best, one of football's all-time greats was brought up on the Cregagh estate. He played for Cregagh Boys' Club before going on to play for Manchester United. At the height of his fame in the 1960s, he was often referred to as the fifth Beatle. *Colour-Rail*

Below: The intersection of Queen Street and Wellington Place, looking towards Donegall Square, the Robinson & Cleaver building, with its tower, prominent in the background. The other tower in the far distance is Belfast Central Fire Station. The building above the shop awning is the Linenhall Library, founded in 1788, the oldest learned institution in the city. The Carlton Restaurant, also seen here, was one of the best-known caterers in Ireland. It was managed by the grandfather of the noted motoring writer, Wilson McComb. Though by the mid-1950s it was obvious that the days of horsedrawn traffic were numbered, some horses remained at work on the streets of Belfast until the late 1960s. *Colour-Rail*

The partially completed liner *Canberra* towers over parked cars at Queen's Island. The *Canberra*, 818ft long and 102ft wide, was the last of the great ocean liners to be built in Belfast by Harland and Wolff. Ordered by the P & O company for their Australian route, she was launched on 16th March 1960 and left Belfast for Southampton on 19th May 1961 to commence her maiden voyage. The development of air travel inevitably led to a decline in business for the great liners and the *Canberra* later became a cruise ship. She also served with distinction as a hospital ship during the Falklands Conflict. The parked vehicles in the foreground include a Series 1 Land Rover and Morris 1000 van. *William Holden*

Great Victoria Street railway station was opened in 1848 by the Ulster Railway, replacing an earlier structure dating from the opening of their line from Belfast to Lisburn, in 1839. Conveniently sited for the city centre, shortsightedly, the station was closed and demolished in the 1970s. In the 1990s common sense prevailed and a new modern rail and bus terminal was built on the site, though in architectural terms a mere shadow of the earlier building. *UFTM AH51*

Left: The McCreary cars were also known as Streamline trams. No 423 is coming out of Queen's Quay station into Scrabo Street. Belfast trams ran right inside two of the city's main railway stations, the Belfast & County Down terminus here at Queen's Quay and the LMS/NCC station at York Road. This sensible but rare feature allowed passengers to transfer between tram and train without getting rained on. The blanking plates on either side below the windscreen show where some of the trams had at one time been fitted with electric indicators. Although the Streamline trams were the newest in the fleet, many of them were scrapped before their predecessors due to structural weaknesses found in the chassis. Only ten of the Streamliners lasted until the closure of the system. *Colour-Rail*

Below: York Road and its railway station with a 1941 AEC trolleybus at the junction with Whitla Street. By 1967 when this photograph was taken, of the former extensive network of the LMS/NCC, only the lines to Larne, Londonderry and Portrush remained open. The station building suffered considerable damage in Second World War air-raids on Belfast. The vehicle parked in front of the station is an Austin FX3 taxi. From 1954, Austin taxis were available with a diesel engine which was immediately extremely popular with operators. The car indicating to turn left is a Vauxhall Cresta. The advertising hoarding in the background is for Cadets cigarettes. *Colour-Rail*

A line of trams are seen in Station Street before the Queen Elizabeth Bridge was built. Tram No 282 and her sisters are waiting in line to pick up shipyard workers at the end of the day's work. The main road out of the city to Bangor goes straight through here now. *Colour-Rail*

Tram No 350 is seen emerging from Ardoyne depot in the north of the city. This large depot, which could hold 84 trams under its Belfast truss roof, was the last tram depot to close. The Belfast truss is a strong light wooden girder made out of small lengths of timber. The supporting lattice allowed large uninterupted spans over areas of up to 90ft to be constructed. They were initially known as lattice girder roofs and were often used in shipyards, railway yards, factories and breweries. They later found popularity as aircraft hangars during the First World War. They were invented and supplied by D Anderson's Lagan Felt Works in Belfast. *Colour-Rail/W. E. Robertson (IR409)*

The old Smithfield market was a popular shopping arcade in the city centre. An Austin Atlantic is parked outside Andrews shop, next door was Montgomery's Pet shop, one of many in the area. Smithfield market was a very popular place with bargain-hunters. Andrews of 60 Smithfield Square had been in business since 1900 and could supply any make of car. They also collected old cars before it became fashionable to do so. The Austin Atlantic was the wildest looking car that the company ever produced. It was aimed at the North American market but failed miserably there, with only 350 cars sold. It was, however, quite successful in Austin's traditional markets. Gold painted instruments gave the dashboard a jukebox feel and options included electric windows, a first for a mass-produced British car. The barber's pole with its red and white stripes is said to represent blood and bandages, dating back to the time when barber surgeons practised medicine, principally blood-letting. *Colour-Rail*

A busy scene at the junction of Royal Avenue and Castle Place. The vehicles include a 1948 Guy trolleybus, a Morris J type van belonging to Robert Johnston Ltd, Motor Accessory Factors, Hardware and Saddlery Merchants of North Street and a Ford Popular van turning right across the path of the trolleybus. A window cleaner, with ladders and bucket, is crossing the road. The 1880s building on the left is the Ulster Reform Club whose members still meet there today. While the street is officially Castle Place, it has been generally known as Castle Junction, a name dating from the time when it was the hub of the Belfast tramway system. It is considered by many as the real centre of the city. *Colour-Rail*

Left: Chamberlain tram No 374, seen at Station Street, is heading for Mountpottinger on route No 51. *Colour-Rail/W. E. Roberston (IR472)*

Right: A Morris 8 follows a 1943 AEC trolleybus on route No 20, Connswater via Queen's Bridge, along Donegall Quay in the docks. This area is now known as Laganside and has changed out of all recognition. *Colour-Rail*

Left: A UTA Leyland bus passes through the wash at Glengall Street bus station adjacent to Great Victoria Street railway station. On the right was another familiar landmark for both bus and rail passengers, the Murray's Erinmore Tobacco building.
Colour-Rail

Below left: A line of trams, mainly Streamliners, with a UTA low-bridge double-decker bus trapped between them, are in Station Street picking up shipyard workers at the end of their day's work. In the early 1950s, when this photograph was taken, the bicycle was a popular and affordable form of transport, cars were still far too expensive for the majority of workers. Station Street took its name from the nearby headquarters and main terminus of the Belfast & County Down Railway whose lines once extended to Newcastle, Castlewellan, Ballynahinch and Donaghadee. By this time the BCDR had been closed down, with the exception of the Bangor branch. *Colour-Rail/W. E. Roberston (IR475)*

Right: A Daimler Fleetline bus, a Mini Traveller and a Morris 1000 are the only vehicles seen crossing the new Queen Elizabeth II bridge. The Heysham and Liverpool cross-channel steamers are tied up at Donegall Quay in the background. The gantries of the shipyard rise up from the Queen's Island. The old railway tunnel which linked the dock lines on the County Antrim side to Maysfield goods yard, where Belfast Cental station now stands, was turned into a pedestrian subway when the bridge was built.
UFTM AH47

Below: Trolleybus No 223 turning into Whiterock Road from Springfield Road on its return journey towards the city centre. The No 11 Whiterock Road route was the last in the city to get trolleybuses in 1959. Other sections of the network had already been abandoned by this time. From its junction with Falls Road, the Whiterock Road climbs steeply. Diesel buses struggled up this hill but the powerful and silent trolleybuses used to fly up it. *Richard Whitford.*

Right: 1948 and 1949 Guy trolleybuses, both with Harkness bodies are entering the grounds of Parliament Buildings at the Massey Avenue gates. These trolleybuses were withdrawn in 1965 and 1966 respectively. Massey Avenue is named after the Rt Hon William Ferguson Massey, a former Prime Minister of New Zealand. Massey was born in Limavady in 1856. He emigrated along with his family in 1870, became Prime Minister in 1912 and served as such until his death in 1925. *Colour Rail*

Left: No 97, a 1943 AEC trolleybus, seen at Parliament Buildings, Stormont, was withdrawn in 1963. This was one of a batch of 114 vehicles ordered in 1939 from the Associated Equipment Company (AEC). When the Second World War broke out the order was reduced by the Ministry of War Transport to 88 vehicles which were delivered between 1940 and 1943. A sister trolleybus, No 98, is preserved unrestored by the Ulster Folk & Transport Museum. *Colour-Rail*

Below: McCreary Streamline tram No 423 at Queen's Quay railway station on a sunny afternoon. The advertisement on the tram is for Cadbury's chocolate, that on the station wall is for the locally-produced, Gallaher's War Horse Bar tobacco. The tram tracks on the left continued into the Harbour Estate and on to the Queen's Road tram terminus. The porte cochere was added onto the front of the station building in 1916 and was removed again before the station was demolished. The letters UT on either side of the clock stand for the Ulster Transport Authority, who ran road and rail services in the province from 1948 onwards. Considered, with every justification judging by its record, a very anti-railway organisation, it was said that UTA stood for Ulster's Track Abandoners. *Colour-Rail*

Daimler fleet No 461 is nearing Carnmoney village and the end of its run. In March 1967, when this photograph was taken, Carnmoney still retained much of its character as a village just beyond the outskirts of the city.

Today shifts in population and residential development have turned Carnmoney into a substantial residential suburb. *Richard Whitford.*

Right: Donegall Place seen from the front of the City Hall with tram No 354, a trolleybus and a GPO van in the foreground. Post office vans of the time had black rubber wings fitted so that minor dents would not show. The trams travelled in the middle of the road, which was fine in the days of horsedrawn traffic. However, it was a distinct drawback when motorised transport became the norm as passengers had to brave the traffic to board and alight from the trams. Trolleybuses and trams used different overhead systems which made for the complicated arrangement of overhead wires at the junction. *Colour-Rail*

Below right: A Garrett traction engine, with a solid-tyred trailer, trundles along Station Street towards Bridge End. It was owned by Harkness, a Belfast haulage firm. The yellow lorry belonged to Samuel Courtney Ltd., paint, varnish and distemper manufacturers and roofing contractors who had premises at 5 Sydenham Road. The shop on the corner of Middlepath Street is Flanagan's Ship Supply Stores. The shop with the 'Players Please' awning was John Foster's confectionery and tobacconist. This whole area has been demolished and replaced with apartments. Only the street names remain. The spire in the background is Saint Joseph's in Sailortown across the River Lagan. It was consecrated in 1879 and closed in February 2001 against the wishes of its 150-strong congregation. *Colour-Rail*

Below: Tram No 350 passing the parish church of St Mark at Ballysillan on its way to the City Hall. St Mark's, a Gothic-revival church, was built in three different phases between 1854 and 1886 by three different architects Lanyon, Lynn and Phillips.
Colour-Rail/W. E. Robertson (IR340)

Right: This drilling platform, *Sea Quest*, was built by Harland & Wolff for BP Oil to search for gas and oil in the North Sea. It was 100ft long and about 320ft high. Each leg was 35ft in diameter. The shipyard's 150 ton floating crane was used in the assembly process. There was room aboard for 63 crew members in berths decorated with colourful melamine plastic veneers and Corlon vinyl linoleum. It was launched on 7th January 1966 and was capable of drilling to a depth of 20,000ft. The cars parked in the foreground include a Mk1 Ford Cortina, an Austin A30, an A35 van, an A50, a Rapier and a Hillman. The little Austins were economical and reliable in the best Austin tradition. They also handled well. Monte Carlo Rally winner and Belfast man, Paddy Hopkirk used to race an A35 at County Down's Kirkistown race track. *William Holden*

Left: A 1963-built Daimler Fleetline bus, No 612, is seen at Donegall Square East with the City Hall grounds on the left. Route No 80 ran via Grosvenor Road and Alliance Ave to Oldpark in the north of the city. 'Model Lemon', advertised on the side of the bus, was a mineral water produced by McKenna & McGinley of Bath Place in the Lower Falls. They also produced a 'Model Orange' flavoured soft drink. *Colour-Rail*

Below: The trolleybus turning circle on the Glen Road in 1967, with St Theresa's Church and Parochial Hall on the left. Belfast was the only city in Ireland to operate trolleybuses. The first route converted, before the war, was the Falls Road, which conveniently had an existing tram depot, at the bottom of the Glen Road, where the vehicles were based. Following the success of the trial, other routes across the city soon followed. The rear roof panel of the trolleybuses was painted dark green as traces of copper from the overhead discoloured the roof at this point. *Colour-Rail*

Top left: Tram No 378 is seen near the top of the Crumlin Road. It is noticeable again here, how far the tram tracks are from the pavement. The lorry belongs to John Morgan & Sons. Builders and Carriers of 155a Oldpark Rd. The Everton school on the right hand side is still there today, and school crossing patrolmen are not as recent an innovation as many people seem to think.
Colour-Rail

Below left: A Streamline tram is seen in College Square East. The cinema to the right is showing *The Ringer*, a 1952 mystery film with Herbert Lom and Donald Wolfit. Herbert Lom is probably best remembered for his portrayal of Inspector Clouseau's insane boss, Chief Inspector Charles Dreyfus, in the Pink Panther comedies. *The Ringer* was the first feature film directed by Guy Hamilton who later directed *The Colditz Story, The Battle of Britain* and many James Bond classics. The Mayfair Cinema was originally named The Kelvin, after William Thompson, Lord Kelvin, who was born here in 1824. He is famous for discovering the two great laws of thermodynamics. *Colour-Rail*

A tub trap with dropped axle passing the Belfast College of Technology. The nearest two cars are a Mk V Jaguar and a 1940s Ford Prefect. The beige car near the statue is a 1950s Ford Prefect. The statue of Dr Henry Cook (1788-1868) is popularly known as 'The Black Man' although this title actually refers to an earlier statue on this site. Parsons & Parsons, gentleman's outfitters is on the corner. These Parsons were related to the Parsons family who had the title the Earl of Rosse. This famous dynasty was of Birr Castle in Co Offaly. William, the 3rd Earl, built the world's largest telescope in 1845 and Charles 'gatecrashed' the Diamond Jubilee Naval Review in 1897 to demonstrate the superiority of his turbine-powered vessel. The sign for estate agents A. Maze & Son remained long after the company had gone. A modern building on the site now houses Northern Ireland's only indigenous building society, the Progressive. *Colour-Rail*

Left: On 14 April 1962, Daimler bus No 254 returns along Sydenham by-pass from Glentoran's Football Ground, the Oval, where Linfield defeated Portadown 4-1 in the Irish Cup Final. Spectators' cars are parked along the central reservation. Glentoran was the first British or Irish team to win a European club competition. In 1914 the team won the Vienna Cup, a competition for national football association cup winners. *Richard Whitford*

Below: Tram No 351 passes through the docks on the County Down side of the River Lagan. Behind the tram are the coal quays. Coal was imported through Belfast and distributed around the country by rail and road. The Ford V8 lorry, to the right of the tram was what was known as a 'forward control' lorry. The driver sat beside the engine rather than behind it, leaving more space to the rear for the load. *Colour-Rail/W. E. Roberston (IR410)*

Below: A 1950 Guy Arab double decker bus parked in Donegall Square South at the rear of the City Hall. Route 64 served Downview, a residential area between Shore Road and the Antrim Road, which had commanding views over Belfast Lough. The unusually tall Belisha Beacon on the extreme right, was necessary to give adequate warning to motorists in heavy city-centre traffic. The rather puzzling advert on the bus reads, 'This bus won't shrink, it has the label-Sanforized'. This referred to a process patented by Cluett Peabody & Co which limited fabric shrinkage to 1%. It was named after its American inventor Sanford L Cluett who was born in 1874 and died in 1968 with over 200 patents to his name. *Colour-Rail*

Right: Trolleybus No 148 negotiates the Dundonald hairpin in the east of the city. This hairpin was part of the triangular race circuit where the famous Ards Tourist Trophy was run from 1928 to 1936. The trolleybus is heading back to the City Hall via the Albert Bridge, from its terminus at Dundonald. The road on the right leads to Comber. The advertisement on the side of the bus is for Lobitos which was a brand of lubricating oil widely used in the 1960s. *Colour-Rail*

Below: Donegall Place and the City Hall on a damp Belfast day. A trolleybus, a Ford 100E and a Volkswagen Beetle are among the few vehicles in sight. The lack of traffic suggests this was a view taken on a Sunday. Small Fords, such as the 100E seen here, had vacuum operated windscreen wipers. The vacuum power was somehow generated by the carburettor, so when you accelerated, the wipers stopped working! Behind the hoarding on the left, Northern Ireland's first Marks & Spencer store was taking shape. The old Gilpin's building on the corner, beside the bus, had been demolished to make way for a modern building occupied by H. Samuel, the jewellers. The familiar outline of Belfast City Hall, forms the backdrop to this view, a building described by John Betjeman as Belfast baroque. *Colour-Rail*

Right: Trolleybus No 198, at the Strathmore Park terminus on the Antrim Road, was one of a batch of 24 vehicles which entered service in 1950. Built by the British United Traction Company, with electrical equipment by GEC, the Belfast firm of Harkness supplied the standard 68-seater bodies. *Richard Whitford.*

Above: A 1957 view of the whitewashed houses of Rowland Street. These workers' houses were built around 1820 when this area was a mill village on the southern outskirts of the city. Originally known as Tea Lane, the street name was changed in the 1880s. It was one of the earliest examples of high-density urban housing for workers flooding into the city seeking employment. These houses were built before bye-laws made compulsory the provision of an enclosed yard with privy and back access so waste from the privy did not have to be carried through the house for disposal. When this area was being redeveloped in the mid 1970s, six houses from Rowland Street were moved and rebuilt in the Ulster Folk & Transport Museum at Cultra. *UFTM AE119*

Right: A city-bound McCreary streamline tram passing the shops on Crumlin Road at the junction with Ardoyne Road just above the roundabout. The tram depot was on the right behind the corrugated iron fence. The rather expensive looking car in the foreground with the impressive radio aerial is a Jaguar. The row of shops on the right is still there, seemingly thriving, with a pharmacy, an off-licence, butchers, bakers, grocers, a post office and take-away food establishments. *Colour-Rail*

Left: Trams queueing up in Donegall Place which is decorated for the Coronation visit by George VI and Queen Elizabeth in July 1937. This offers a rare colour view of the livery carried by Belfast trams before the blue and cream became commonplace. The second tram from the front, a balcony car, is in the earlier red and cream colour scheme. This car's advertisement suggests that Ty-phoo tea is a remedy for indigestion, a claim which would surely not be made today.
Colour-Rail/William Robb MBE (IR474)

Below: No 531 turning from Cherryvalley Gardens into Cherryvalley Park on its way back to the city centre, in April 1965. Cherryvalley, a middle-class residential suburb to the east of the city, has suffered more than its fair share of undeserved ridicule and mockery over the years. Cherryvalley ladies were pilloried as the epitome of exaggerated gentility and politeness. *Richard Whitford.*

Left: The Great Northern Railway V class compound 4-4-0 locomotive No 85 *Merlin,* arrives for preservation at the former Belfast Transport Museum, on a low loader hauled by a Northern Ireland Carriers' Scammell. Chater Street, which ran along the rear of the museum, was the last cobbled street in the city. When the Museum was moved to Cultra the cobbled street surface was left behind where it still remains. Chater Street was entirely destroyed on 5 May 1941 by German bombs during the Blitz. The Harland & Wolff crane *Goliath*, is visible beyond the embankment, now removed, which once carried the main line of the Belfast & County Down Railway. The museum building in Witham Street, is now home to Clements Chemicals. All the terraced housing in view has been replaced with modern housing. *Robert Beggs*

Below: Streamline tram No 440 at Wellington Place with the Athletic Stores on the left. The Austin A40 Devon car was registered in Northampton borough. When introduced in 1947, Austin proudly announced, 'Colour comes back to motoring', as the cars were available in maroon, grey or light green. The car is turning left into Queen Street. *Colour-Rail*

Left: 1947 Daimler double-decker bus No 277, fitted with Harkness bodywork, heads down Botanic Avenue towards the city centre passing a much more modern Daimler bus, a 1963 Fleetline, on route No 83 to Ormeau. The cars parked in leafy Botanic Avenue that day include a Mini Traveller and a Triumph Spitfire. *Colour-Rail*

Below: Car No 349 climbs the steep incline on Ligoniel Road above its junction with Crumlin Road in the north-west of the city. The pillars on the right mark the boundary of Glenbank Park. The houses in the picture are still there today and remain very well-kept. Most of these fine villas have names, a practice common in residential suburbs. *Colour-Rail*

Left: Trolleybus No 207 was citybound on route No 13 from the Glen Road, when it broke a spring at Beechmount Drive on the Falls Road and had to be towed back to the depot. The Falls Road route was always one of the busiest routes, not just because it served a relatively densely-populated part of the city, but because it also served the Royal Victoria Hospital, the Royal Maternity Hospital and the Royal Hospital for Sick Children. *Richard Whitford*

Below: Chamberlain tram No 383 at the junction of Queen's Road and Sydenham Road in the Harbour Estate, looking in the direction of the Dee Street bridge. Some of the Chamberlain trams, including this one, were built in Belfast. The vantage point from which the photograph was taken is now occupied by the service entrance of the Odyssey, an entertainment and conference centre built to celebrate the Millennium, Belfast's answer to the Greenwich Dome! *Colour-Rail*

Left: Donegall Square North with Chichester Street stretching into the distance and the City Hall grounds on the right. The Titanic memorial is still in its original site in the middle of the road. It has since been moved to within the grounds of the City Hall. The metallic red car is a Citroen Traction Avant. The street surfaces are still cobbled apart from the section in front of the City Hall. For many years the pavement corner in front of the City Hall was the traditional stand for flower-sellers. *Colour-Rail*

Below: A 1943 AEC trolleybus heading out of the city on route No 31 to Castlereagh, at the Conway shop on the corner of Castlereagh Road and Orangefield Crescent. The shop has been replaced by apartments but the garage is still there, run by Nigel McFarland Auto Services. Singer Van Morrison attended Orangefield Boys School. As part of the group, 'Them', Van played regularly at the Maritime Hotel opposite the City Hall in the early 1960s. The Maritime had been popular for dance and variety shows since the mid-1940s. One of the most colourful characters to play the venue was Sam Mahood, front man for 'Just Five'. The Maritime may be gone but both soul legends Sam and Van are still performing. *Reg Ludgate*

Below: Streamline tram No 397 descending Ligoniel hill in 1953. In the 1800s this had been the main road from Belfast to Lough Neagh. The trams on this road were kept busy bringing workers to and from the mills on the hill. The whitewashed houses have now all been demolished and the small boys watching the progress of the tram will probably be looking forward to retirement shortly. The large red brick building on the left hand side of the road is Ligoniel Methodist church. *Colour-Rail*

Right: The tanker *Orcoma,* docked at Belfast, was built in 1966 by Harland & Wolff for the Nile Steamship Company as a tanker for vegetable oil. She was 508 feet long and 70 feet wide. The parked cars include a 100E, a Ford Escort estate car, a split-screen Morris Minor, a Ford Consul, a Morris Oxford and a Morris Traveller. *William Holden*

Below: Tram No 364 at the corner of Queen's Road and Channel Road carries an advertisement for Harcourt's coal. Harcourts were a major coal importer and Sir John Harcourt was Lord Mayor of Belfast from 1955 to 1956. Ireland has virtually no indigenous coal so most of the coal used in Northern Ireland was imported through Belfast docks. The building being roofed in the background is part of the Harland & Wolff shipyard. This area is close to the Oddyssy Centre. *Colour-Rail*

Right: In the post-war years the change over from trams to trolleybuses and omnibuses was resumed. In 1950 the Corporation's transport fleet comprised 249 trams, 210 trolleybuses and 190 omnibuses. This 1949 Guy trolleybus, No 168, is on driver-training duty at Strathmore Park. The advert is for Denny bacon and sausages which are still enjoyed in the city. This vehicle is now preserved at the Black Country Museum at Dudley in the West Midlands. *Colour-Rail*

Top left: Chamberlain tram No 381 at Ballygomartin Road. The advert on the gable wall in the background is for Wilton's Funeral Parlour, at Nos 245-249 Crumlin Road with branches at 2 Wheatfield Gardens and 227 Ballygomartin Rd. The company still exists today. The building with the gable facing the street to the left of the tram is Forth River Primary School. The scene is little changed to this day. This view is looking towards the city with Glencairn housing estate immediately behind. The rope for adjusting the trolley pole is noticable in this view. Mason's Paint advertised on the tram, is still available today. It was a popular paint with many transport companies, so the whole tram may be painted with Mason's.
Colour-Rail/I. Davidson (IR526)

Below left: A 1954 BUT trolleybus and diesel double decker bus. The red brick building in the background is the headquarters of the Belfast Education Authority in Academy Street. The Corporation Transport Department had a driving training school on the Lisburn Road, where all the old tram drivers were turned into trolleybus drivers. The course took three weeks. The first stage was theoretical and was carried out in a classrooom where there was a full scale replica of a trolleybus cab with wheel, brakes and switches. Then the pupil was taken out in a diesel bus fitted with fluid flywheel and pre-selector gears, and coached in steering, acceleration and reversing. Finally they were moved onto a trolleybus and put through final training before becoming qualified.
Colour-Rail

Trolleybus No 210 turning from Chichester Street into Victoria Street in August 1963, at the start of its run to Cregagh. This manoeuvre would be impossible today with the one-way traffic arrangements. Victoria Street used to be known as Cow Lane, because the residents of Ann Street and High Street would daily drive their cows out to pasture at May's Fields. When Queen Victoria and Prince Albert visited Belfast to open the newly-cut Victoria Channel, the city fathers changed the name lest Her Majesty suffer the indignity of being driven along Cow Lane. *Richard Whitford*

Below: In this July 1964 view, a blue Mini is crossing Shaftesbury Square to Donegall Road with the Ulster Bank's new premises in the background. Elizabeth Frink's aluminium sculpture 'Airborne Men' on the bank caused some controversy and not a little bemusement. Between the Mini and the bank was one of a pair of underground Victorian public lavatories, the green railings of its counterpart can be seen to the right. A Ford Anglia 105E is entering the square from the Dublin Road, once the main southerly exit from the city. *UFTM F135*

Right: Trolleybus No 193 at the Grove turning circle on the Shore Road to the north of the city. This turning facility was only used occasionally when, for example, there was a diversion on the route or short working. The Grove Baths swimming pool can be seen in the right background. The Baths opened in the 1960s and for many years was the only facility in Ireland able to hold major swimming competitions.
Richard Whitford

Castle Street looking towards Castle Place. The travel agency on the left is in part of the Commonwealth House building. The illuminated advert on the roof-top is for Younger's Monk Pale Ale. Cars visible include a MkII Ford Cortina, a Volkswagen Beetle, and an Austin Cambridge. Sawer's Delicatessen and the Norwich Union Insurance Society offices are on the right. The MkII Cortina was introduced in 1966 and in 1967, the year that this photo was taken, the Cortina was top-selling car in the UK for the first time. Anderson & McAuley's department store is the building on the right beyond Fountain Street, which joins Castle Street behind the trolleybus on the right. In the early 1950s, Fountain Street was home to the Embassy Club, the only night club in Ireland. The club had been popular with American servicemen during the war. On Fridays it was open from 9pm to 3am. There was a teenagers' club on Wednesdays and Saturdays where 'hot' rhythm and 'Bebop' fans filled the dance floor. Their telegraphic address was 'success'. *Colour-Rail*

Tram No 345 passing the gate lodge of Ligoniel Villa, the residence of the manager of Ligoniel Spinning Mill. The gate lodge, or porter's lodge as it was referred to locally, has gone but the boundary wall is still evident and the gate is now an entrance to Ligoniel Park. The tram is just leaving the Ligoniel terminus for the City Hall via the Crumlin Road. These were excellent trams which gave good and reliable service until the tram system closed in 1954. The gate lodge marked the boundary of the city.
Colour-Rail

A 1954 BUT trolleybus at the Co-operative store on Shore Road. The Co-op is now Sandra's Nursery Corner. The top of Seaview Church can just be seen above the trolleybus. The photographer is standing by Seaview football ground, the home of Crusaders Football Club. This service from Whitewell, is working through to the Falls Road.
Colour-Rail

Tram No 389, en route for Ligoniel is passing over the Queen's Bridge. The bridge was built in the 1840s to a design by Woodhouse and Frazer. It was widened in 1885 with the footpaths cantilevered out at the side and the distinctive lampposts, with a dolphin motif were added. The tram is about to pass the premises of George Cohen & Company Limited, a large firm of iron, steel and scrap metal merchants. *Colour-Rail/W. E. Robertson (IR343)*

This 1944 Daimler double decker bus, fleet No 198, registration GZ 1578, gave the city many years of service. It was photographed at Glengormley Boy Scout hall in 1970, the year it was withdrawn. On this occasion No 198 was on private hire, an enthusiasts' outing for the Irish Transport Trust, on a showery Sunday morning. *Colour-Rail*

On the eastern side of the city, the change over from trams to trolleybuses on the Cregagh, Castlereagh, Stormont and Dundonald routes took place during early 1940s. Here a 1948 Guy trolleybus climbs the incline to Parliament Buildings, Stormont from the Massey Avenue entrance. The red brick building is Campbell College set in its 130 acre estate. Founded in 1894, Campbell College is one of the most famous private schools in the Belfast area. The writer Samuel Beckett taught at the school for a short time. It is reputed that when the headmaster asked him if he was aware that the school's students were, 'the cream of Ulster', Beckett agreed that they were indeed the cream, 'rich and thick'. Belfast has many excellent schools and it is still considered a good place to be educated.
Colour-Rail

Tram No 364 passing the Water Office in Donegall Square North. The advert on the tram is for Christies, a wallpaper and paint business. Alderman [later Sir] William Christie was Lord Mayor of Belfast for three years from 1972 to 1975. The green railings in the roadway behind the tram mark the entrance to underground toilets. The middle of a wide road or other open space was favoured by Victorian engineers for siting public conveniences, the land was already in public ownership and the toilets could be ventilated into the open air. The turret roof appearing over the tram is on a building at the corner of Callender Street which is now occupied by the Bradford & Bingley Building Society. The tower in the distance is at Chichester Street Fire Station. It was used for training and for the drying of hosepipes after use. *Colour-Rail/W. E. Robertson (IR342)*

Trolleybus No 218, at the turning circle on the Whitewell Road. This vehicle was supplied by British United Traction in 1954 and fitted with a Harkness body. It was withdrawn in 1968, the year after this photograph was taken. After London, Belfast had the largest trolleybus fleet in the United Kingdom and was the only one in the whole of Ireland. In the background is Cave Hill shrouded in cloud on this wet day. The building is Throne Primary School, since demolished. Hazelwood Integrated school now occupies the site. *Colour-Rail*

Below: A Streamline tram passes a branch of The Fifty Shilling Tailors, one of the early chain stores, at the junction of Royal Avenue and Castle Place. A shoe shop is now on this site and the building next door has been rebuilt as a modern post office. The advert on the tram is for *Radio Times*, still a best selling weekly magazine after all these years.
Colour-Rail/W. E. Robertson (IR473)

Right: The leading vehicle, No 246, a Sunbeam trolleybus was the newest in the Belfast fleet, entering service in 1958. Seen here on Stewart Street heading to Haymarket Depot on Saturday 11 May 1968. No 246 is now preserved in England at the East Anglia Transport Museum, at Carlton Colville, near Lowestoft, by members of the London Trolleybus Preservation Society. Kennedy's bread vans, one of which is parked on the left of the picture, were a familiar sight around the city. A popular street rhyme applied to all the city bakers was and not just this firm ran, 'Kennedy's Bread - Sticks to your belly like lead'! *Colour-Rail*

Tram No 123 turns from Donegall Square North into Donegall Place. This car was a rebuilt vehicle with a body made by the Service Motor Works of Belfast. An Ulster Transport Authority Luton body furniture removal lorry, probably a Commer (though the UTA also used vehicles supplied by Leyland, Scammell and Bedford) is on the far right of the picture. The car to the left of the UTA lorry is a Morris 8.
Colour-Rail/Reg Ludgate collection

Trolleybus No 183, seen in East Bridge Street, is heading for the nearby Haymarket depot. Behind the bus is St George's Market. This was designed by the City Surveyor, J C Bretland, and built in the 1890s to house the sale of butter, eggs and poultry, and finally fruit. There was also in this vicinity a Cattle Market, a Pork Market, a Fish Market, a Horse Market, and as the name of the trolleybus depot suggests, a Hay Market. The restored St George's Market is the last remnant of the many markets which gave their name to this part of the city. *Richard Whitford.*

Below: Double decker buses, mainly Daimlers, shelter from the rain at the Falls Road Depot. The third vehicle from the left, Harkness bodied No 356, dating from 1952, was withdrawn due to malicious damage in 1970. The depot has a Belfast truss roof. The depot was accidentally burnt down on 1st March 1966 but was quickly rebuilt. This was the home of Belfast's first trolleybuses which were introduced on the Falls Road routes before the Second World War. Falls Road depot remains a busy Citybus garage to this day. *Colour-Rail*

Right: Streamline car No 406 at Queen's Quay is advertising Gilpin's of North Street, 'the shop for men'. Gilpin's had several clothing shops in the city. The Custom House is in the background, behind is one of the cross-channel steamers which docked close to the city centre. *Colour-Rail*

Below: This is the building used by Ulster Television, at Havelock Place, on the Ormeau Road. This one-time shirt factory became, and remains, the headquarters of UTV which first broadcast on 31st October 1959. Favourite early local programmes included the topical daily magazine programme 'Roundabout', the children's programme 'Romper Room', hosted by Miss Adrienne and later by Miss Helen and a request programme presented and performed by Tommy James, 'Teatime with Tommy'. An important milestone in the company's development was the opening in 1962 of a £100,000 TV station extension, seen on the right of the photo. The following year the station's programmes became available to a much wider audience with the opening of the Strabane transmitter which served the west of the province. The confectioner's shop in Havelock Street was run by Alex Chambers, who had no doubt, had many famous customers. The parked cars include an Austin A40, a Morris 1100, a 3-litre Rover. a Mini van and a Mini, all popular in the 1960s. *Wilfred Capper*

Right: A Streamline tram and an Austin A40 van race around the corner from Wellington Place into College Square East. The Ulster branch of the Overseas League occupied 31 Wellington Place. The car parked round the corner in Wellington Place is an Armstrong Siddeley. The red shop on the corner, long gone, was the Belfast Gold Exchange, Jewellers, of 64 Wellington Place. *Colour-Rail*

Left: The curved neo-classical terraces of Upper and Lower Crescents, near Queen's University, were built between 1846 and 1852 by James Corry. Among the few cars parked on Upper Crescent, as a woman brushes the pavement outside her home, are a Vauxhall, an Austin A30 and a Morris 1100. *UFTM F17*

Below: Tram No 388 approaches the corner of Station Street and Bridge End. There was a double junction here so that trams on rush hour extra workings provided for shipyard workers, could travel directly to and from east Belfast without having to reverse or pass through the city centre. John Kelly, one time owners of 29 steamships and Ireland's largest coal importers, had their head office in Station Street.
Colour-Rail/W. E. Robertson (IR412)

Below: A 1948 BUT trolleybus is at the turning circle at Casement Park on the Andersonstown Road on 14th May 1967. Trolleybuses were first introduced on the Falls Road in 1938. This Harkness-bodied vehicle lasted until the end of service in 1968 when the trolleybuses were replaced with diesel buses. The Ford Zodiac, seen on the right, was the top of the range Ford car of the time. The Zodiac Executive, introduced in 1965, featured such luxuries as a push-button radio and seat belts. These cars starred in the BBC TV police series of the time, Z Cars, which also featured the Belfast actor Jimmy Ellis who played Sgt Bert Lynch. *Colour-Rail*

Right: Four trolleybuses at the Cregagh terminus in April 1963. The Cregagh route was first converted to trolleybus operation in 1941. Since this photograph was taken the area has changed considerably. No longer is this location on the very edge of the city and there has been considerable development beyond the former trolleybus terminus in the last 40 years. The turning circle is, however, virtually unchanged. *Richard Whitford*

Below: A 1949 Guy trolleybus heading out of the city on the Belmont Road. Stewart Johnston's garage at 203-205 Belmont Road is no longer there, the site is now occupied by Kingsley Court, a cul-de-sac consisting of apartments. The MS sign stood for a local oil company, Munster Simms. This company was engaged in the oil trade as long ago as 1879 when it began to import lamp oil in wooden barrels. The car on the left is a Standard tourer and a big Riley RM is city-bound in the distance. The trolley poles are gone but all the other houses, gateposts, road surfaces and gratings remain. *Colour-Rail*

Right No 112, an 1948 Guy BTX trolleybus is seen in Royal Avenue heading towards Castle Junction and the City Hall on an enthusiasts' trip in May 1968 before the system finally closed. The white building is the Grand Central Hotel and just beyond is the city's main Post Office. This entire block has been re-developed and is now the Castle Court Shopping Centre. This trolleybus is now preserved by the Ulster Folk & Transpot Museum at Cultra. *Colour-Rail*

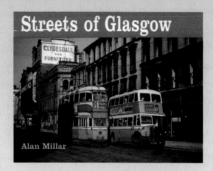
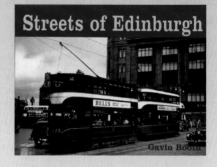